I0435035

Survival Preppers
Doomsday Survival Checklist

Prepare Professional Survival & First Aid Kits for Your Home, Bunker, Auto, Work, and Bug-Out Bag

By David Presnell
www.SurviveUntilTheEndComes.com

Warning and Disclaimer

This publication is designed to provide accurate and authoritative information with regard to the subject matter covered. However, the author is not a doctor, lawyer, accountant, or other professional. This publication is sold with the understanding that the author is not engaged in rendering medical, legal, financial, accounting, or other professional advice. If medical advice or treatment, financial services, or other expert assistance is required, the services of a competent professional person should be sought. This publication is sold with the understanding that the author cannot accept responsibility for any injuries, loss, or damage that may result from the use or misuse of following any of the text or information contained herein, nor be liable for legal prosecutions that may arise as a result of following any information contained in this book. The material herein is provided for informational and entertainment purposes only. If you should use any of the information in this book for any reason, you do so entirely at your own risk.

Any trademarks used in this book are the property of their respective owners.

www.SurviveUntilTheEndComes.com

Table of Contents

Introduction

The days of chaos are upon us... The day of reckoning is at hand!

If you are a survival prepper, a survivalist, or someone just thinking about how to protect yourself and your family from the coming hell on earth then you need this "Survival Preppers Doomsday Survival *Checklist*". This comprehensive survival and first aid checklist was carefully put together and field tested for over eight years during the development of the book *"Survive Until The End Comes".* It includes three complete lists for home or bunker, auto, and personal or travel for both survival and first aid. From it you can construct the perfect survival and medical disaster preparedness solutions. From it you can put together, in a moment's notice the perfect bug-out kit, or auto kit. Having a prepared list to go by will be of tremendous value when a survival event occurs. Leaving one thing out may reduce your chances of survival.

One of the primary principles I wished to encourage in my survival book "Survive Until The End Comes" (www.SurviveUntilTheEndComes.com) is the ability to improvise. You must learn how to make do without any possessed supplies, including first aid and survival kits. The chances are high that you may not have any prepared first aid kits available to you when the survival event first occurs. You must also learn how to quickly become self-sufficient in a survival situation, because, sooner or later, your supplies will run out. You must learn how to depend totally on yourself to survive without any prepared or stored supplies, first aid kits or help from the outside. Preparing your professional survival and first aid kits now will help you know exactly what supplies you will need to look for when a survival event occurs.

Of course, if you are near your automobile, office, or home during a survival event, having well-prepared professional first aid kits, survival kits and a good bug-out bag at your disposal can make your ability to survive much easier and surer. Should you have professionally designed first aid kits, survival kits, and the training to use them? Absolutely! They will be valuable to you in any emergency situation at home, on the road, and at work. Can you do them yourself? With these lists you can! Preparing from these lists should help you dramatically increase your chances of surviving any situation. Leaving one vital piece of survival gear out of your plans could be the difference in life and death. This checklist will help you become properly and professionally prepared. Are you ready?

Chapter 1: Survival Kits

I suggest three types of survival kits: primary home or bunker kit, auto kit, and personal or travel (bug-out) survival kit. The home kit is the most extensive and the one you will most likely use in an extended survival event. This is the kit you will depend on to get you through the power going out, the food supply ending, and possible total chaos after the event occurs. At a minimum, your primary kit should get you through thirty days to six months. The auto survival kit is a basic version designed to keep you alive until you get to your primary home kit. It's the one you keep in the trunk of your car. A personal survival kit is the one you may wish to carry in a day pack with your travel or personal first aid kit. This would be your bug-out bag. The personal (bug-out) first aid kit is a minimum list only. You should add any other items you may need as the situation demands.

A work survival kit is optional, but it may be a good idea for you to discuss this with your employer. A work kit (not listed) should be similar to the home kit but smaller and customized to your work environment.

The primary home or bunker survival kit lists consumables such as food and water "per person." Multiply the quantities listed by the number of people you expect to use your survival kit.

Listed are suggested quantities only. You do not have to go out and purchase all these items at once. Like your first aid kits, just build them up a little at a time. You may want to include more or less of some items. You may wish to exclude the large items that you may not have space for, such as the generators. Store your primary home survival kit in one or more new large plastic trash cans or plastic storage containers with new trash bags in place. When full, seal the top of the bag and place the lid on tightly. Store some of your supplies in clean five-gallon buckets with a rubber seal removable lids. Should the need arise, one of the large trash cans can be used just outside for waste disposal, while one of the five-gallon buckets (with a bag) can be used as a toilet. Containers can be just as important as the contents during a survival event, especially water and fuel containers. Some of the large items can simply be stored on shelves in your basement or pantry or in the top of a closet.

Your auto survival kit can be put together from your home kit and can be replenished as needed. You might include it with your auto first aid kit and place both in a good waterproof bag which is placed into a plastic bucket (five-gallon if you have room for it) with a lid to keep in the trunk of your car.

Personal or travel survival kits, also known as "bug-out" kits (see "bug-out" discussion below), can be quickly put together on an as needed basis. You can place the necessary items into a day pack depending on the day's survival needs. If you are going in search of food for only a few hours, then your first aid and survival kit requirements may be basic. However, if you are traveling for many days or leaving the area for good, then you will likely carry a fully-equipped heavy pack with water filtration, sleeping gear, and all the other necessary survival gear (personal weapons, waterproof cold weather clothing, and good hiking boots for example) for long distance traveling. The personal survival kit is a basic version designed to get you through the first 72-hours.

Be sure you test out each item you purchase to be sure that it will work during a real survival event. Test food, too, from time to time. Be sure to check expiration dates and rotate often. Keep your stocks as fresh as possible. Change out your water from time to time, as well. If you have trouble finding some of the supplies mentioned below, check my website occasionally at www.SurviveUntilTheEndComes.com for updates and information on some of the supplies as they become available. Get a copy of *Survive Until The End Comes"* and practice, practice, practice survival techniques until you are comfortable with the basic methods. A magnesium fire starter is of no value unless you can start a fire with it in the pouring rain. Practice filtering water, making shelter, and making yourself invisible to potential harm. Learn to properly identify, prepare, and try edible wild foods. Anybody can find food in the middle of summer, but what about in the middle of winter? Learn and practice how to survive.

My Notes:

Primary Home Survival Kit

[ ] 30-Day Supply (30 gallons per person) of Drinking Water. Drinking water must be distilled, boiled, or sealed bottled water to be used only for drinking or cooking. Allow one gallon per person per day. Clearly identify this water as use for drinking only.

[ ] 30-Day Supply (40 gallons) of Clean Non-Drinking Water. This water can be from the tap and stored in 5-gallon water jugs. Use for washing and other sanitary needs. Might be boiled or filtered or chemically treated and used for cooking or drinking only if from a known safe source. Make your supply last at least thirty days. Allow forty gallons per person for thirty days.

[ ] Water Containers. These would be included in the above water storage, but be sure the containers or jugs are sturdy enough to be reused. Once the event is over, you may have to walk and carry drinking water from long distances. Camping suppliers have 5-gallon blue water containers that work well for storage and have sturdy handles. Good ones are heavy duty plastic cubes with spigots, can be stacked several high, and cost under $10 each.

[ ] 30-Day Supply of Non-Perishable Food. Allow two complete meals and one snack per person per day. Be sure to think about portions. Keep your portions correct and you will not have the problem of leftovers or wasted food. With no electricity and no way of refrigerating your food, you probably want to avoid leftovers. Be sure to consider storage containers for leftover items such as crackers. Food will be too valuable to waste. Also consider heavy-duty plastic plates, spoons, forks, knives and plastic food storage bags of several sizes. MRE's and freeze-dried meals work great for your auto and personal or travel kits, but canned and long-term dated packaged food will serve you well for your home or bunker storage.

[ ] Primary Home or Bunker First Aid Kit (discussed above)

[ ] (2) 16' x 20' Heavy-Duty Nylon Reinforced Tarps. These have so many uses that I

will not even mention them. Well, I'll mention two. Your roof was blown off by a severe thunderstorm. Rain is pouring in your house and you know that your insurance will not pay for water damage. These tarps can seal some large holes and protect your valuable belongings until permanent repairs can be made. You may also want to have a good ladder that will reach your roof should the need arise. Another reason for the tarps is that you can shelter your entire family in two of these quite well. Even if you use a tent, it is a good idea to put a tarp under and over it if you really want to stay dry. Don't forget rope to tie off the tarps.

[ ] 100 Feet of 3/8-Inch (or (4) 25-Foot Packs) Polypropylene or Nylon Cord for Tarps or Other Uses

[ ] 25 - 50 Feet of Heavy-Duty Polypropylene Rope with a Minimum 300-Pound Working Strength. There are too many possible uses to list. Get the rope.

[ ] (2) Rolls 10' x 25' Six-Mil Heavy-Duty Plastic Sheeting. The roll size may vary, but be sure you have enough to cover all the windows and doors of your house. You may also want to include a staple gun and staples with this plastic so you can quickly staple it up. When the power is out and the temperature drops or rises drastically, this plastic can help keep your space livable. Sealed with duct tape, such plastic window and door covers can reportedly help protect you from some chemical and biological hazards. This plastic can also be used to make temporary emergency shelters, collect rain water, make a solar still, make a hot bed for seeding plants, create an emergency chemical suit and more.

[ ] Family-Size Tent. If you put one of these in your kit, set it up every few months to air it out and keep it in good shape. Be sure to put it away dry and as suggested by the instructions that come with the tent. If you properly care for this tent, it will last for years.

[ ] Sleeping Bag Rated to at Least 15°F (lesser degree if you live in a cold climate) Oversize rectangular are the most comfortable, but mummy-style are usually warmer. For extended stays, I prefer the oversize rectangular bags that unzip all the way around. They can be used as a large comforter, as well. These bags do not have to be

expensive; just be sure they are rated to at least as cold as your typical coldest winter temperature in the area where you live. You will need one full-size sleeping bag per person (including children). Never buy children-size bags. Your children will outgrow them. Plus, full-size bags have a higher barter value.

[ ] (4) Wool Blankets. Acquire new military issue or good quality military surplus and have them dry-cleaned and wrapped in a plastic bag to keep them clean and dry. You will need four blankets per person. Good quality wool is your best choice. It will keep you warm even when damp.

[ ] Rain Suit Made of Vinyl or Rubber Including Pants (preferably with suspenders and bib pants and a full-length coat with hood.) Be sure these fit loosely enough to wear clothes underneath. You will need one suit for each person. These suits should be heavy-duty and good quality. They can be used for protection from the elements such as rain or snow, or for use during biological or radioactive events. Put a small roll of duct tape with each suit.

[ ] A Biological / Chemical Suit for Each Person (like used in hospitals)

[ ] Rubber Gloves. These should be heavy-duty, long gauntlet-style for use with rain suit above. You will need one pair for each person.

[ ] Rubber Boots. These must be heavy-duty, slip-on, all rubber or vinyl boots with no buckles or zippers, with at least twelve-inch tops and traction soles. You will need one pair for each person.

[ ] Solar Shower (5-Gallon)

[ ] (4) Filter Masks N95 (designed to be used by an automotive body painter. Get a good one that will filter pesticides and smoke particles). Get one or more for each person. These are inexpensive and made mostly of paper. (See "Primary First Aid Kit" above).

[ ] (1) Full-Face Military-Style Gas or P100 Chemical Mask for Each Person. (Filters at least 99.97% of airborne particles and is strongly resistant to oil)

[ ] Hard Hat (with Winter Liner) for Each Person

[ ] (4) Rolls (Minimum) of Waterproof High Quality Mil Spec Duct Tape. This has so many uses. I will probably list it several times. You can get this from your hardware store or a military surplus store, but beware of cheap import versions. You can use it for repair or to seal your chemical suit to your boots, gloves, and face mask. You can use it to seal around your windows and doors or just to hold things together. In an emergency, you can use duct tape to attach a splint or hold a pressure dressing onto your injured leg.

[ ] Spare Clothes and Shoes. Long-sleeve shirts, pants, socks, boots, and underwear should be included as a minimum. The best is wool or wool blends for outer clothes. If you live in cold country, include: insulated underwear, heavy winter socks, insulated boots, coat or parka, headgear, and gloves or mittens. Be sure to include clothes for each person. Remember, loose-fitting clothing is better than tight-fitting clothing. These can be items you normally use and would keep in your closet or other normal place. When an event occurs, you should gather and put these items together for emergency use or travel. That's why this checklist is so important. Your ability to gather the things you need quickly and completely will be very important, especially if you have to get out of the area.

[ ] Knives. You will need a good high quality 7-inch or 8-inch hunting knife and sheath. I suggest getting the best quality you can afford. Many good quality sheath knives are available at large camping supply stores for around $40. This is a knife that you may carry on your belt. You should also have a good heavy-duty web or leather belt to carry this knife on. This is your primary survival knife. You will use it for many tasks, including cooking and possibly protection. You will also need a good multipurpose pocket knife. I suggest a Swiss Army® style that has two cutting blades, a saw blade, and other attachments such as screwdrivers and scissors. Some have corkscrews. I must admit, I've never had the need to use a corkscrew, but I suppose if you are the survivor of a major disaster and you happen upon a bottle of corked wine, a corkscrew could be of

real value. Your smaller knife will be used almost daily. Think about how many times a day you use some type of knife. Be sure these two knives are in your survival kits. You will also need a good sharpening tool. I have a lot of experience using whetstones, but you do not need to learn that skill. The simplest way to sharpen your knives is with a carbide knife sharpener. The oldest one I have is made by Ecko®. I purchased it from a rack of kitchen utensils at the local hardware store when I was a teenager. It has eight wheels (four on each side) that runs inside it and has a plastic handle. You simply drag the knife blade through the center of the wheels a few times to get a good edge. Versions of these are still available for a few dollars. These will get the job done, but it is best if you learn how to properly sharpen your knives with whet or oil stones and steel (the old way) and keep them razor sharp.

[ ] Multi-Tools: Include one or more of the famous Leatherman® (or other good brand) folding pocket-style, multipurpose tools. The better ones of these include a large and small knife blade, pliers, saw, screwdrivers, scissors, file, and punch. I suggest a large one and small one in each survival kit. The prices have come down, but it is still good to get the best quality you can afford. Don't waste your money on cheap imitations. They are worthless for most uses.

[ ] Fire-Starting Kit. The minimum items to include in your home or bunker fire-starting kit are three large boxes of strike-anywhere wooden matches (sealed in plastic bags), eight good quality BIC® disposable butane lighters, four magnesium fire starters, four packs of fire-starting sticks (usually ten or twelve sticks per pack), three Zippo®-style fluid and flint type lighters, three cans of lighter fluid and a pack of extra flints for the Zippo® (these old-style lighters can use different fuels—with caution—and work quite well on windy days). I advocate the use of BIC® butane lighters. I have one that has been in one of my backpacking survival kits that I have had for over twenty years. It still works and I have used it to start many fires. Don't waste your money on cheaper brands.

[ ] Cooking Kit. As a minimum, your home or bunker cooking kit should contain a high quality stainless steel family mess kit. Be sure and don't be cheap here. If you cannot find a good family mess kit, you should have two good 4-quart and 6-quart stainless steel pots with tight-fitting lids (preferably ones with wire hoops or strong steel handles), a large stainless steel frying pan, a large kettle-type pot that will hold a gallon or better, and a good stainless steel coffeepot with well-fitting lid and fireproof handle. Most of

these can be found in the camping section of your favorite department store, just don't buy cheap junk. If you cannot find stainless steel, you might be able to find heavy aluminum pots and pans from a military surplus store. Do not buy nonstick coated pans. They will not hold up over a fire. Do not buy anything that feels lightweight or cheap. If you can bend the metal with your thumb, it probably will not hold up under daily survival use. Cast iron is fine if you can deal with the weight and cost. You will also need at least two good stainless steel plates and two large stainless steel cups for each person. You will need two sets of eating utensils (spoons, forks, knives) for each person. Two sets allow one to be awaiting washing while the other is being used. Both sets are washed at the same time, saving water. You should also include two plastic insulated cups with lids for hot or cold liquids. You will also need a good set of cooking utensils, forks, tongs, turners, and gloves. The kind used for grilling is fine. Wood or plastic handles can create cleaning problems with potential bacterial growth. Use all stainless steel utensils. Include a couple of good glove-type fire mitts or grilling gloves and potholders. Include a box or two of the good quality square toothpicks. They will be worth much more than you can imagine during a survival situation. In your cooking kit, you should include three sealed small cans of shortening. It's better to use the small cans with resealable lids than opening one large can. You can also include a large bottle of cooking oil such as canola or corn oil. Be sure and check the "use by" dates at least once every three months on all food items. In your cooking kit, you should also include a portable way to cook your food. In this kit you should include one-burner and two-burner propane stoves. These stoves use the small disposable propane cylinders available almost anywhere. The single burner stove screws directly into the cylinder. The two burner version has a hose that connects to the cylinder. I suggest both stoves because they are inexpensive and one could fail. When you only need to warm a cup of water, the single burner will save fuel. When you need to cook a meal, you may use all three. When you put a cylinder on a stove, provided there are no leaks, do not remove it until it is empty. Just cut it off completely when finished cooking. Removing it and placing it on other devices will waste fuel. Liquid-fueled (multi-fueled) stoves are not really economical for short-term survival, and they are much more dangerous since you have to fill them with liquid fuel and pump to pressurize. However, multi-fueled stoves may provide benefits over long-term survival situations since you can use white gas and kerosene in some brands (read the instructions carefully). You should stock at least twelve propane cylinders in your home or bunker survival kit. Read the directions that come with your stoves and carefully follow all instructions, warnings, and cautions about their use, including dangers of using indoors. Proper ventilation should always be used with any device that burns something to get results. Include salt, pepper, sugar, and any of your favorite spices in your cooking kit. Please don't forget things like a manual can opener, bottle opener, a good butcher knife, and a carbide knife sharpener. You will also need some dishwashing liquid and cloths, some scouring pads, and a can or two of Ajax® type powder cleanser.

[ ] Fishing Kit. Put a good basic fishing outfit in your survival kit. A Zebco® 33 (or equivalent) rod & reel is perfect for most creek fishing. Be sure you have extra line, hooks, sinkers, and snap swivels. Most of these reels come with a lightweight line. I also suggest you get a roll of 20-lb test line for setting hooks. You could also stock a trot line and cast net and an extra two-piece rod.

[ ] Traps and Snares: You will need good quality rat and mouse traps, steel snares for small and large game, steel traps for small and large game, and snare and trip wire for predators including potential human intruders.

[ ] Portable Battery-Powered AM/FM Radio (with two extra sets of fresh batteries). A good digital shortwave with AM/FM is even better.

[ ] Portable Battery-Powered Weather Radio or Police Scanner (with weather frequencies plus two extra sets of fresh batteries). These are generally better than the AM/FM combinations that have to be manually tuned in.

[ ] A Solar AAA through D Battery Charger. Get one that works. Avoid cheap flea market types.

[ ] Flashlights. You should have a heavy-duty waterproof flashlight that uses D batteries and a heavy-duty waterproof 6-volt battery-style lantern with two sets of fresh dated batteries for each. I like the Energizer® hard case flashlights. I have used them in downpours and have dropped them several times and they still work. The three D-cell nightstick-style aluminum flashlights are fine provided they are good quality. I also like the small two AA cell waterproof aluminum flashlights for up close use. They usually come with a belt holster. Be sure you have at least two extra sets of fresh dated batteries for all your battery-powered equipment. You can buy bulk packs; just be sure and buy

the best quality, such as, Energizer® alkaline or Duracell® alkaline. Check the "use by" dates when you buy them, and check them at least every three months to be sure the batteries are not getting old. Rotate them with fresh batteries when the date gets close and use up the old ones. I suggest you buy your batteries from a place that sells a lot of batteries. If a retailer sells many batteries, they are likely to have them with "use by" dates many years in the future. Never buy batteries from flea markets or discount centers. You get what you pay for, and your life may depend on what you buy now and in the near future. The new 200 lumen and above flashlights are great for defense purposes, but for long-term use tend to use up the batteries much faster than traditional bulb types, but's it your preference. Test your flashlights with different batteries to see how long they will burn with alkaline versus heavy-duty cells and different brands. You might be surprised. Never buy cheap off-brand batteries. You'll regret it.

[ ] Lantern (not battery operated). A good choice is the propane dual mantle camping lantern that screws directly into a standard disposable propane bottle. You should have three extra propane bottles and four extra packs of mantles that fit your lantern. The pump-up multi-fueled lanterns are efficient, but more difficult and dangerous to operate, and are subject to failure from faulty pumps and clogged needles. Old-style kerosene lanterns with wicks are efficient but more dangerous. If tipped over or dropped, you can be sure of a serious fire. If you use either the pump-style or wick-style, you will also have to store the proper liquid fuel and keep it fresh. You should also stock spare parts for the pump lantern.

[ ] Portable Heaters. I recommend two types. One is popularly known as Mr. Heater®. This, or an equivalent brand, is available at almost all department or hardware stores. It operates for several hours on a standard 16.4-ounce disposable propane bottle and can be used indoors with the small bottles. If you purchase an adapter and hose kit, which I recommend, you can connect it directly to a standard 20-pound propane cylinder like you use with your gas grill. These put out 4,000 to 9,000 BTU/hour. Be sure and carefully follow all directions that come with your heater. Mr. Heater® also comes as a dual-burner heater that puts out up to 18,000 BTU/hour. I also suggest that you have a name brand kerosene heater designed to be used indoors. The round types are better than the rectangular kind. Be sure you get a high quality 'UL listed®' model with all the safety features. Follow the directions, carefully, and learn how to safely use and maintain the heater before you need it. Never fill a kerosene heater indoors or when it

is hot. Never use any other type of fuel except what the manufacturer recommends. Allow it to cool completely and take it outdoors to fill it. If you spill kerosene while filling, wipe up the spill. Be sure you have proper ventilation. You must never use any heater in an enclosed space. Fresh air must be introduced into the area to prevent the buildup of carbon monoxide which can kill you quickly. Properly used, these round kerosene heaters can provide around 20,000 BTU/hour of safe heat. They can heat a small home in an emergency. Most hold around five gallons of kerosene, and will burn from four to eight hours per fill-up. Storing fuel can be hazardous, as well. It must be stored outside the home and maintained in a fresh state. If you have a safe place away from your home to store kerosene such as a secure outbuilding, you may want to keep five 5-gallon jugs of kerosene on hand. You can add fuel stabilizer designed for kerosene to help keep it fresh. These stabilizers are sold under various trade names. Be sure to purchase a stabilizer made especially for kerosene. There are special containers for kerosene that clearly state "Kerosene" on them. Never put kerosene in gasoline containers. If you blow yourself up, then that defeats the entire purpose of survival. Use caution with flammables and stay alive.

[ ] Candles. Stock a good supply of high quality hurricane candles and safe holders. These are available in camping supply sections of most department or sporting goods stores. Don't buy the long, slim classic candles used at weddings or for dinner tables. They are too tall to be safe, and they do not last very long. Pint or quart jar candles can be used, but I don't recommend them. They are more for decorative purposes. Often the jar candles will burn down just so far and put themselves out due to the puddle of melted wax. Candles should provide light and some heat. Don't buy scented candles. They may be irritating to some people. I like a product I have used while camping known as a "Candle Lantern" and other brand names. These lanterns hold the hurricane candles and protect them from wind. They make the candles burn more efficiently. A dozen hurricane candles can get you through a week of power outages during those nighttime and early morning needs.

[ ] Special Personal Needs such as Prescription Medications or Other Medical Needs. Be sure to have an extra pair of prescription and reading glasses. Try to maintain a thirty-day emergency supply of prescription medications and keep it freshly dated. Talk to your doctor about obtaining these for you. Be sure to keep a check on expiration dates and rotate your prescriptions.

[ ] Portable Chemical Toilet and Extra Chemicals. These are available in camping supply sections of most department stores for around $50. They are a great item to have when the power goes out. Read the directions and learn how to use yours. You can also purchase a seat designed to fit a 5-gallon bucket. Just drop a 13-gallon trash bag or a bag specially-designed for this use in the bucket, attach the seat, use it, and remove the bag and properly dispose of the bagged goodies. Please don't fling these in your neighbor's backyard. They may attract dangerous animals and cause disease. The best thing to do is bury them and cover with dirt. If you own a portable chemical toilet, be sure and follow the manufacturer's directions for safe use.

[ ] Personal Sanitation and Hygiene Items. You need to stock thirty rolls of toilet paper per person. This should give you a thirty-day supply. You need four boxes of facial tissue per person, two sealed containers of moist wipes per person (these will dry out in storage so rotate them often with replacements and use the old ones before they dry out), and four rolls of high quality paper towels per person. Stock any feminine hygiene needs such as tampons or sanitary pads that would last at least one week. Stock personal items for each person's likes, such as: underarm deodorants, aftershave lotions, body powders and sprays, one dozen disposable dual-blade safety razors, several bars of antibacterial soap, talcum powder, petroleum jelly, toothbrushes, toothpaste, and a large bottle of mouthwash. I would also put two washcloths, two hand towels, a small bar of antibacterial soap, and a large bath towel in your kit for each person. These can be placed in a plastic pail or 2-gallon bucket (with snap-on lid) that can be used as a portable sink; one bucket for each person. Get quality buckets. Cheap buckets will break up easily. Another nice item to include in toiletries is a good plastic cup for each person. Survival does not require you to have bad breath or body odor. These items will have a high barter value too, in time.

[ ] Don't Forget the Little Ones and the Elderly. You may need date checked formulas, extra prescription medications, hearing aid batteries, dentures and denture cleaning solutions, as well as, diapers, bottles, toys, pacifiers, and other needs for infants and the elderly. Don't forget extra eyeglasses (possibly an old but still usable pair), contacts and contact lens solutions.

[ ] Survival Rifles, Pistols, and Ammo (if trained and experienced in their use). A .22 caliber rifle with a good accurate scope is probably the best for small game. A bolt-action hunting rifle is best for larger game. Be sure to buy good quality ammo. Everybody has their own idea about defense and hunting weapons. My first suggestion is to stick with the most common calibers that would be used by the military such as 9mm or 45 caliber for defense pistols, 223 Rem for defense, 308 for a good bolt-action for hunting. This ammo should be more available than some specialized rare round. My next suggestion is to learn how to use your weapons and practice often.

[ ] Survival Hunting Bow & Arrows or Crossbow (train and become experienced in their use).

[ ] Signaling Devices. This could include whistles, flare guns, signal flares, signaling mirrors, or other attention-getting devices.

[ ] Bottles or Packs of Potassium Iodide Tablets (65mg or 130mg) (also in first aid kit).

[ ] Binoculars and a Good Tripod-mounted Long Range Spotting Scope with Range Finder

[ ] Extra Pair of Vision or Reading Glasses

[ ] Protective Devices and Equipment. These could include items like weapons that you are licensed, trained, and skilled to use; (fighting knives, clubs, pepper spray, tasers), fire extinguishers and other firefighting equipment; protective clothing and other specialized equipment such as radiation detectors, gas detectors, burglar alarms, and other such devices. This equipment is up to you and your personal skills. As far as weapons, my thoughts are that if you do not know how to properly use them, they may be more of a danger to you than any potential protection they may seemingly provide. Also, see list in "Primary Home First Aid Kit".

[ ] Money. There is an entire chapter in *"Survive Until The End Comes"* about what may

be used as money during a real long-term survival situation, but it would be a good idea to put a few dollars in your survival kit, as well as, some U.S. 1964 and earlier 90% silver coins. I would suggest enough cash to pay all your bills for at least one month. Be sure to include enough to cover rent or mortgage payments, electric bills, grocery bills, and fuel bills. Power cut-off notices were sent to homeowners who missed their payments during Hurricane Sandy. The mail ran, but the power was not on, so how could they cut it off. Some of these people didn't even have homes to live in. The cut-off notices kept coming. That's just a thought for future consideration. These companies will expect their money on time no matter what is going on. Do not forget to cover the basics such as money for food and water, shelter, and fuel for heating and cooking.

[ ] Color Copies of Your Personal Identification Cards (including driver's license, birth certificates, social security cards, and other identification). You should have these copies laminated to protect them from moisture. Legally, you may have to have these items enlarged 200 percent when copied. If you lose your originals or should they get destroyed, you will have something to prove who you are. If you do not believe this can happen, just review some of the news stories that evolved from Katrina about lost identity. You may also want copies of all insurance policies or any papers that may prove your financial standing at banks or brokerage firms. Try to have all your copies of identifying papers notarized for legal use (especially birth certificates).

[ ] Digging and Trenching Tools. A small, good quality, folding military-style shovel and pick would be good to have. A good quality full-size round point shovel would also be useful, as would an old-style mattock or pick-style digging tool. Be sure to get good quality steel.

[ ] Cutting Tools. You will need a good bow saw. You might also include a good woodsman-style single-bit ax. Learn to use it safely. A chainsaw is good if you are experienced in its use and can store fuel. A good quality twelve-inch bow saw that comes with both metal and wood-cutting blades can be purchased for around $30 at most camping supply stores. These are excellent for cutting wood for the fire and through the bones of any recent deer kills; just change the blades. The metal-cutting hacksaw blades work just fine on meat and bones. You will need a good quality 6" – 8" folding saw for your other kits too. Saws are as vital as knives in survival situations.

[ ] Generators. I recommend two. One is a portable 1850-watt gasoline powered generator that will run several hours on a fill-up. These are the kinds you see powering lights and televisions at campgrounds. My small generator will run a computer, a Monitor oil stove, a color television, and a small AA battery charger, but not all at the same time. It will not run a refrigerator or freezer or table saw with any dependability. There is just not enough wattage. My other generator is a 5500-watt semi-portable on a frame with wheels. This small generator will run a freezer and a refrigerator but not both at the same time. It is great for plugging up to the freezer or refrigerator and running an hour or so until the freezer or refrigerator has cooled to a normal inside temperature. If you fire up your generator within an hour after a power outage, you should be able to maintain internal temperatures by running your generator a few minutes every two hours, or until your fuel supply is gone. If you have generators, you must also store clean, stabilized fuel in a safe place. Read and follow all safety precautions and instructions that come with your generator. Never run a generator inside an enclosed space. Carbon monoxide can kill you from running a generator in an enclosed space. Run them outdoors. Follow the manufacturer's instructions, carefully. You will need a good heavy-duty drop cord to run the power into your home or shelter. The power from your generator can kill you just like the power from an electrical outlet in your home, so use with care. My thoughts about generators are simple. If the power is out for a day or two, maybe up to a week, a generator and a good safe supply of fuel can keep your cold food cold, your frozen food frozen, and keep you from freezing to death. If the power goes out indefinitely, such as during a nuclear war, the generator would only be useful to keep your cold food fresh until you could eat it up or prepare it for storage by canning or other storage methods. After that, your generator would be valuable for pumping drinking water out of wells and running fuel pumps to pump fuel out of underground tanks. Such a generator would have to be protected. If you happen to be the only one in town with a generator during such a long-term event, many other people would want what you have, and some may seek to take it and your fuel from you. Your life might become worth exactly the price of that generator and the fuel to run it. If such a long-term event should occur, the generator and fuel would be a good way to gradually transition from the luxuries of life, such as electricity, to a simpler way of candles and wood fires. This slower transition period might help reduce some of the stress caused by the event. My theory about generators and other items that must be supplied or filled up regularly is that we must learn how to prepare to live without them. Simply having them in our possession may increase the risk of someone trying to take them away from us by force. If you are prepared to return force with greater force, then you may be able

to keep your "highly-prized consumable items" for a little while, but usually someone comes along who desires your items more than you do. By consumable items, I mean those that have to be supplied, such as something that uses gas or bullets. Once the supply of gas is gone a car is worthless, unless you can find someone with a supply of gas. Once the supply of bullets is gone, a gun is worthless, unless you can find someone with a supply of bullets. If you happen to be that person with a good supply of gas and bullets, you may be able to barter them for food, or, you may just die trying to protect them. If you purchase generators, learn how to use them. Run them until you know how to use them properly. Be sure to break them in properly and service them as suggested in the instructions. Learn what you can and cannot power with your generator. You need a fuel efficient generator big enough to run your refrigerator and freezer. A large generator for the whole house that uses five gallons of fuel per hour would not be efficient over the long-term.

[ ] Telephone. Get a "non-battery operated" plug-in, slim-style, touchtone telephone. These are usually available for under $10 at department or electronics stores. The problem with portable telephones is the fact they do not work when the power is out. Our local telephone company has had service during every power outage, provided you had a phone that operated entirely on the line voltage. Only two wires are actually used on most of these simple phones. If you are handy you can make an adapter with alligator clips that will allow you to clip your phone directly to a line box.

[ ] Compass and Topographical Maps (of the general area you live in). Purchase a good quality waterproof glow-in-the-dark type compass. Learn how to set up a map and how to use your compass to get from point A to point B. The directions that come with your compass will tell you how to properly orient and use it. Learn how to read topographical maps. You may never need either, the maps or the compass; but for a few dollars, each can be in your survival kit. These are especially important in your home and office survival kits.

[ ] A Good Watch with Hands, Day, and Date. It may bring you much comfort. You should also have an extra fresh battery. You might even find an old working wind-up or automatic type ideally waterproof and shock proof. It will probably survive an EMP, too.

[ ] Wire. Buy a roll of piano wire, or similar wire that is thin and hard to break. Also get a roll or two of soft 18- or 20-gauge tie wire. A roll of twist tie wire might be of value as well. You may also want to include a roll of 18-gauge electrical wire. You should also have two 50-foot, heavy-duty drop cords besides the ones you have with your generators. When the power goes out, the need for wire will become evident. You may need to make snares, trip wires, tie things up, repair things, and so on. You may need to divert any available electricity to areas where you need it with 'UL Listed®' insulated electrical wire and drop cords.

[ ] A Notebook, Pen, Pencils and Sharpener. You may want to write about your adventures. It will help pass the time, and should you find the survival event over and you have survived, you just might be able to sell your story to a publisher.

[ ] Survival Manual (Get a copy of *"Survive Until The End Comes"* and learn and practice often).

[ ] Repair Kit. A good repair kit should include the following items: good quality scissors, tweezers, adhesive duct tape, electrical tape, filament tape, pliers, wire-cutting pliers, Phillips- and flat-head screwdrivers, a roll of nylon 20-pound test fishing line, 72–inch shoestrings, a small knife, safety pins of various sizes, a roll of tie wire, a 500-foot roll of nylon cord (nylon bricklayer's line), tire repair kit for tube and tubeless tires, plumbing repair kit with assorted washers, tube of Super Glue, bottle of contact cement, tube of silicone adhesive, and a high-quality sewing kit for both clothing and heavy-duty sewing, such as canvas. Be sure to include regular and darning thread, regular and heavy-duty needles, and a variety of buttons.

All these items don't have to be stored as a unit; they could be stored around the house and used as needed. In the event of an emergency, they can be pulled together to be more accessible. You may already have many of these items in your house. It would be a good idea to identify them and make a list, so you would have ready access to them in the event of the emergency. Remember the gear is only as good as your ability to use it. Learn about and practice using every piece of equipment you have. Learn how to properly maintain, sharpen, and repair your equipment including generators and saws. Learn how to make water safe to drink. Learn how to construct shelter where none seems to exists. Learn how to make fire in poor conditions. A shovel that breaks during its first use or matches that will not strike are worthless. Get the best quality you can. Make sure your gear will work as intended when needed. When you need it, your life may depend on it.

Custom Additions To This List:

[ ] _____

[ ] _____

[ ] _____

[ ] _____

[ ] _____

[ ] _____

[ ] _____

[ ] _____

[ ] _____

Auto Survival Kit

[ ] 5-Day Supply (5 Gallons) of Drinking Water. Drinking water must be distilled, boiled, or sealed bottled water to be used only for drinking or cooking. Allow one gallon per person per day. The 5-gallon blue plastic water containers will stow in most trunks easily and in back out of the way.

[ ] (5) Meals Ready to Eat (MRE's-with heaters per person)

[ ] Auto First Aid Kit (as described earlier)

[ ] (1) 16' x 20' Heavy-Duty Nylon Reinforced Tarp

[ ] 50 Feet of 3/8-Inch (or two 25-foot packs) Polypropylene or Nylon Cord for Tarp or Other Uses

[ ] 25 - 50 Feet of Heavy-Duty Polypropylene Rope (with a minimum 300-pound working strength)

[ ] Sleeping Bag Rated to at Least 15ºF - per person (colder if you live in a cold climate or during winter travel)

[ ] (1) Wool Military-Style Blanket - per person

[ ] Rain Suit Made of Vinyl or Rubber including Pants, (preferably with suspenders and bib pants and a full-length coat with hood). Be sure these fit loosely enough to wear clothes underneath. You will need one suit for each person. These suits should be heavy-duty and good quality. They can be used for protection from the elements such as rain or snow, or for use during biological or radioactive events.

[ ] Rubber Gloves. These should be heavy-duty, long gauntlet-style for use with rain suit above. You will need one pair for each person.

[ ] Rubber Boots. These must be heavy-duty, slip-on, all rubber or vinyl boots with no buckles or zippers, with at least twelve-inch tops and traction soles. You will need one pair for each person.

[ ] (1) P100 Filter Mask for Each Person (filters at least 99.97% of airborne particles and is strongly resistant to oil)

[ ] Solar Shower (2-5 Gallon)

[ ] (1) Roll Duct Tape (waterproof high quality mil spec)

[ ] Spare Clothes and Shoes. Long-sleeve shirts, pants, socks, boots, and underwear; minimum. The best is wool or wool blends for outer clothes. If you live in cold country, be sure to include: insulated underwear, heavy winter socks, insulated boots, coat or parka, headgear, and gloves or mittens. Be sure to include clothes for each person. Remember, loose-fitting clothing is better than tight-fitting clothing. You may have to spend several nights in your car while making your way home.

[ ] Knives. Include one 7-inch or 8-inch hunting knife and sheath and a Swiss Army® pocket knife.

[ ] Folding Saw (6-inch - 8-inch good quality name brand).

[ ] Multi-Tools: Include one or more of the famous Leatherman® or other name brand, folding pocket-style, multiple purpose tools. The better ones include a large and small knife blade, pliers, saw, screwdrivers, scissors, file, and punch. I suggest a large one and small one in each survival kit. The prices have come down, but it is still good to get the best quality you can afford.

[ ] Fire-Starting Kit. The minimum to include in your auto fire-starting kit is a plastic Ziploc® bag with a dozen strike-anywhere wooden matches (sealed in waterproof match containers), two good quality disposable BIC® butane lighters, one magnesium fire starter, one pack of fire-starting sticks for tinder (usually ten or twelve sticks per pack) and two hurricane candles.

[ ] Small Backpack Style Mess Kit

[ ] Portable Fishing Kit. This should include a small roll of 20-lb test line, assorted size hooks, sinkers, and snap swivels.

[ ] Flashlights. You should have a heavy-duty waterproof flashlight that uses D batteries or a heavy-duty waterproof 6-volt battery-style lantern with an extra set of fresh dated batteries in the trunk of your car. The three D-cell nightstick-style aluminum flashlights are fine provided they are good quality. I also like the small (two AA cell) waterproof aluminum flashlights for up close use. They usually come with a belt holster. Be sure you have at least two extra sets of fresh dated batteries for all your battery-powered equipment.

[ ] Special Medical Needs (such as prescription medications or other medical needs).

[ ] Personal Sanitation and Hygiene Items. A pack of travel toilet paper from the camping section of your favorite store is a must have. One roll of high-quality paper towels should also be included.

[ ] A Good Vehicle Fire Extinguisher; a Pair of Jumper Cables; a Small Tool Set (including sockets designed for your automobile); a Plug Type Vehicle Tire Repair kit; Two Cans of Tire Sealer/Inflator; a 12-Volt Portable Air Compressor; Tire Gauge; Spare Belts for Your Vehicle Engine; Heavy Work Gloves; Road Flares; Small Fuel Container (empty) and Siphoning Hose. This equipment is up to you and your personal skills.

[ ] Signaling Devices. This could include whistles, flare guns, signal flares, signaling mirrors, or other attention-getting devices.

[ ] Binoculars

[ ] Extra Pair of Vision or Reading Glasses

[ ] Money

[ ] Color Copies of Your Personal Identification Cards, (including driver's license, birth certificate, social security card, and other identification. Ideally, have these copies laminated to protect them from moisture).

[ ] Power Inverter 12-Volt

[ ] Compass and Topographical Maps (of the general area you will be driving through)

[ ] Small Roll of Tie Wire, Snare Wire, and Roll (minimum 100lb test) Bank Line

[ ] A Notebook and Pencil

[ ] Survival Manual

For an auto survival kit, you would simply pull a few of the most important items from your basic home kit and bag them up in a backpack or duffel bag; place them in the trunk of your car with your auto first aid kit. You would need enough items to get you through a few hours up to a few days or until you could get home. Think about the items you may need to get from your place of work to your home if a disaster occurred. Use common sense. You probably would not need a full five-day food supply, but you could need a good topographical map of the area between your workplace and home. The ability to build a shelter, build a fire, and secure fresh clean water and food should be required in any survival kit, as should the items necessary to keep you from freezing to death if you have to stay overnight in your car.

Custom Additions To This List:

[ ] _____

[ ] _____

[ ] _____

[ ] _____

[ ] _____

[ ] _____

[ ] _____

[ ] _____

[ ] _____

The Perfect Bug-Out Kit

I suppose this is a good place for a discussion on the recently famous "bug-out bag". Many people ask me, "What's the perfect "bug-out" kit?" My response usually goes, "Exactly what are you "bugging out" from?" That usually gets some funny looks and then they ponder the question. "Bug-out" kits seem to have become a craze for people selling survival supplies. The idea exists that there is a small backpack that contains every possible thing you would need to survive any situation that you may encounter while "bugging out". That is neither logical nor possible. If the question is pushed, my answer will always be, "The best "bug-out" kit is the knowledge and experience you have in your mind. This and other survival books should provide adequate knowledge. You will have to develop your experience by testing and practicing survival methods under controlled conditions until you become comfortable applying them. Once you acquired knowledge and practiced skills with survival, then you might consider construction of three good first aid kits for your home, auto, and travel as discussed in detail earlier in this list. You might also consider constructing three good survival kits for your home, auto, and travel. We have covered the home and auto survival kits and will get to the personal travel or "bug-out" kit shortly. Once you have knowledge, skills, and supplies on hand, ask me the question again. My answer would be, "It depends! What are you "bugging out" from?" The entire book *"Survive Until The End Comes"* and especially the chapter on traveling and emergency shelters answers that question. Read this book. In it, you will find the answer to the perfect "bug-out" kit question. Every so called "bug-out" kit would be constructed on an "as needed per situation" basis. Every "bug-out" kit would be custom constructed to fit the particular situation you are in and the skills of the user. What are your primary concerns and needs? Do you need fire on the trip? Will you need a water filter? Will you need weapons? Will you need overnight gear? For a good general "bug-out" kit, find a good day pack, place the personal travel first aid kit in it and proceed to read the lists and descriptions given below for the personal travel survival kit. You will be able to put together the perfect "bug-out" kit just for you. Check out my website for the latest information: www.SurviveUntilTheEndComes.com.

Personal or Travel Survival Kit

The personal or travel survival kit is a fully customizable lightweight kit that contains more compact items not necessarily included in the home and auto kits. The kit listed below is a basic kit. Personal or travel survival kits, also known as "bug-out" kits (see "bug-out" discussion above) can be quickly put together on an as needed basis. You can place the necessary items into a day pack depending on the day's survival needs. The secret to creating a personal survival kit is the knowledge you have between your ears. The more you understand about survival, the easier it will be for you to assemble a good survival kit. A premade "bug-out" kit is of little real use. The personal survival kit listed below is a basic version designed to get you through one night or 24 hours.

[ ] Drinking Water. 20-oz heavy plastic bottles work well and can be reused. Carry as many as you think you will need for the day's work and possibly overnight.

[ ] Portable Backpack-Style Water Filter (MSR Sweetwater Water Purifier is my recommended filter – filters down to 0.2 microns and kills 99.99% of the bad things in water).

[ ] Meals Ready to Eat (MRE's) with Heaters. Allow two complete meals and one snack per person per day. Be sure to think about portions. Keep your portions correct and you will not have the problem of leftovers or wasted food. With no electricity and no way of refrigerating your food, you probably want to avoid leftovers. Be sure to consider storage containers such as Ziplock® plastic bags for leftover items. Food will be too valuable to waste.

[ ] Personal or Travel First Aid Kit (see above)

[ ] (2) 10' x 12' (or larger) Waterproof Lightweight Nylon Reinforced Tarps

[ ] 100 Feet of 1/4-Inch (or four 25-foot packs) Polypropylene or Nylon Cord for Tarps

(or other uses)

[ ] (2) Large 55-Gallon Size Heavy-Duty Trash Bags

[ ] 25 - 50 Feet of Heavy-Duty Polypropylene Rope (with a minimum 300-pound working strength) or 100 Feet of Real 550 Military Para-Cord with a 550-pound break strength

[ ] Sleeping Bag (optional)

[ ] Small Pocket-Size, Foil-Type Survival Blanket (reflects body heat) or Heavy Duty Tarp Version

[ ] (2) Wool Blankets (optional)

[ ] Poncho (extra-large waterproof, heavy-duty coated nylon with grommets)

[ ] (1) Paper N95 or Higher Filter Mask (P100 is best)

[ ] Small Roll Duct Tape (waterproof high quality mil spec)

[ ] Extra Clothes and Shoes (depending on prevailing weather)

[ ] Fixed Blade High Quality Large Hunting Knife and Sheath (8" - 12" long with minimum 1/8" thick blade). You will also need a good multipurpose pocket knife. I suggest a Victorinox® Swiss Army Hunter XT that has a locking cutting blade, locking serrated cutting blade with gut hook, and a saw blade and Phillips screwdriver. These are larger and longer than traditional Swiss Army® knives. They have a better grip and usually come with a case.

[ ] Multi-Tools: Include one of the famous Leatherman® or other name brand, folding pocket-style, multiple purpose tools in your personal survival kit. The better ones of these include a large and small knife blade, pliers, saw, screwdrivers, scissors, file, and punch.

[ ] Fire-Starting Kit. The minimum to include in your personal fire-starting kit is strike-anywhere wooden matches (sealed in waterproof match containers), two good quality disposable BIC® butane lighters, one magnesium fire starter, one pack of fire-starting sticks for tinder (usually ten or twelve sticks per pack), two hurricane candles and two tea light candles all contained in a large zip-up plastic freezer bag.

[ ] Small High-Quality Backpack-Style Cooking Kit and a Small Butane or One-Burner Propane Stove. You could also include a small manual can opener and bottle opener and a few feet of aluminum foil.

[ ] Fishing Kit (including several yards of 20-lb test line, some assorted size hooks (size 2, 4, and 6 are good for most small fish), small sinkers, and snap swivels)

[ ] Electronic Communications Equipment and Batteries (optional)

[ ] Flashlights. One of the small (two AA cell) waterproof aluminum flashlights and an extra set of batteries is a minimum. They usually come with a belt holster. I also like the new rubberized or aluminum high output (over 100 lumens) lights. These are also available in AA battery-size. These can be used to temporarily blind an attacker too.

[ ] Special Medical Needs (such as prescription medications or other medical needs)

[ ] Personal Sanitation and Hygiene Items

[ ] Extra Pair of Vision or Reading Glasses

[ ] (2) Packs of the Small Portable Toilet Paper Rolls

[ ] Sunblock (SPF 30 or Higher)

[ ] Insect Repellent

[ ] Survival Rifle, Defense Pistol and Ammo (if trained and experienced in their use). (A .22 caliber with a good accurate scope is probably the best for small game. A bolt-action hunting rifle in 308 caliber is one of the best for larger game. Be sure to buy good quality ammo)

[ ] Survival Hunting Bow and Arrows or Crossbow (If trained and experienced in their use)

[ ] Signaling Devices. This could include whistles, signaling mirrors, or other attention-getting devices.

[ ] Good Quality Folding Saw

[ ] Light Stick

[ ] Compact Good Quality Binoculars (optional but well worth its weight if scanning the area for food or danger)

[ ] Protective Devices and Equipment. These could include items like weapons that you are licensed, trained, and skilled to use; protective clothing and other specialized equipment, such as radiation detectors, gas detectors, and other such devices. This equipment is up to you and your personal skills.

[ ] Money and Barter Items

[ ] Personal Identification Cards

[ ] Digging and Trenching Tools (optional)

[ ] Cutting Tools such as Gerber® Gator Combo Ax with Saw (optional)

[ ] Compass (and GPS & Batteries if desired) and Topographical Maps (of the general area you will be traveling through)

[ ] A Good Watch (remember, an EMP should not affect an old-style mechanical watch)

[ ] Wire. Buy a roll of piano wire, something thin and hard to break. Also, get a roll or two of soft 18- or 20-gauge tie wire. You may need to make snares, trip wires, tie things up, repair things, and so on.

[ ] A Notebook and Pencil

[ ] Survival Manual – Best to study and practice survival skills and plant them in your brain so you will respond instinctively when an event occurs.

[ ] Portable Repair Kit. A good repair kit should include the following items: good quality pair of small scissors, tweezers, a few feet of adhesive duct tape, a few feet of electrical tape, a few feet of filament tape, a roll heavy-duty dental floss, 72–inch shoestrings, safety pins of various sizes, a few feet of light gauge tie wire, a 100-foot piece of nylon line (nylon bricklayer's line), a high-quality pocket-size sewing kit for both clothing and heavy-duty sewing, such as canvas. Be sure to include regular and darning thread, regular and heavy-duty needles, and a variety of buttons.

The personal or travel survival kit listed above is basic. Think about the items you may need to get to where you are going and back to your shelter. Allow for at least three extra days beyond what you think your kit will need. Use common sense. You will have to customize your personal survival kit to fit the needs of the situation at hand. The ability to build a shelter, build a fire, and secure fresh clean water and food and defend yourself from potential threats would be required in any survival kit.

Custom Additions To This List:

[ ] _____

[ ] _____

[ ] _____

[ ] _____

[ ] _____

[ ] _____

[ ] _____

[ ] _____

[ ] _____

Chapter 2: First Aid Kits

Most cheap, department store variety first aid kits are designed for small cuts and bruises and include some over-the-counter pain pills and other such items. They usually have a small first aid booklet, a few various sized Band-Aids® and small bandages and a roll of tape. Some of the more expensive ones include scissors that will barely cut, tweezers that will barely remove a splinter, and some added drugs and ointments such as burn cream, painkillers, and other types of miracle cures. These kits were probably never designed for real life-and-death medical emergencies, but rather home non-emergency first aid use. It's almost like buying an Easter basket. You pay for a real fancy package with very little candy inside. The same is true of most cheap store-bought first aid kits. You get a nice box. The stuff inside is not worth the price. However, within the aisles of the medical supplies section of the drug store or department store where you find these first aid kits are most of the necessary medical supplies you will need to build a real first aid kit; one you could depend on in a real emergency. Of course, you can purchase first-class professional first aid kits and professional emergency response kits used by emergency medical professionals, but they will cost you an arm and a leg. If you can afford these, fine. If you wish to save some money, then build your own, and learn how to use everything in it.

Before starting your first aid kit, get enrolled in first aid classes, and possibly, an Emergency Medical Technician class. Once you start learning about true medical emergencies and how they are dealt with, you will learn what you need and how to use it. Also, once you become familiar with how ambulances and "emergency medical response kits" are stocked, you will know how to put yours together for easiest use. You may also be able to get supplies at or below cost from your instructors to help stock your "emergency response bag" or first aid kit. You may be able to get some slightly out-of-date or overstocked supplies for free. Instructors will show you all kinds of fancy gadgets that they have; some good and some almost worthless. You will learn all kinds of fancy names for first aid kits and the stuff that goes in them.

Most good first aid kits are contained in a good box or bag. For the money, it is hard to beat a good large floating tackle box or large waterproof tackle bag used for fishing. If you purchase a box, don't get the two-sided type. They will dump your supplies. Get the large traditional double-lid top-opening style. When the tops are opened out, trays come up and out of the box on each side. You have a large storage area in the bottom, as well. You really don't want anything removable such as trays. They will get left out, and when you need what is in the tray, it will not be in the box. We used a heavy aluminum version of these boxes specially made for medical use when I worked with Medical Rescue. They could take a lot of abuse and held plenty of supplies cleanly and very organized. If you cannot afford this type, a top-opening single lid with hinged trays is the next best thing.

The next choice is a large waterproof tackle bag (or duffle bag) that is top-opening and not full of small boxes. The bags are less organized and do not protect your supplies from crushing damage as well as the plastic or metal ones. You may also want to look at the large backpacks made for cameras and lenses. These can be converted to medical bags quite readily, and, provided they are large enough, make your first aid kit very portable. Most of these backpack style camera bags are waterproof. Regular size heavy-duty backpacks can also make adequate portable first aid kits. Be sure to look at and study the ones used by the first responders, EMTs, and paramedics where you are taking your first aid training. See what they like and dislike about theirs.

Your largest container will become your primary home kit. If money is short, it can simply be contained in a large plastic storage container with a waterproof lid, such as, a new trash can or several five-gallon buckets. I also want you to make smaller versions for each car trunk and one for use in your travel or bug-out kit or at work.

These can be placed in much smaller bags, ideally waterproof, zippered, and just large enough to hold the contents. You will be making three types of first aid kits: the primary kit and smaller ones that are actually extensions from your large kit. The smaller kits are designed to get you home to your larger stash of supplies or travel with you to your bug-out destination.

Once you have a container for your "primary home (or bunker) first aid kit," you can start assembling it. The primary kit will contain enough supplies to work with multiple injuries and multiple people. You can supply your smaller single-use kits from this one (except for specialized items); however, be sure if you use anything from the kits, replace it within a day or it will not be there when you need it. Check the date on everything at least every six months. Items that are not dated should be carefully marked with a date when purchased and should be checked for quality, regularly.

Check batteries and lights to be sure they work and are not corroded. At the same time, check for moisture damage and mold. It's a good idea to have a printed list with the original inventory written on it and the "use by' dates so you can check to see if anything needs to be replaced. Be sure to ask your first aid instructors about obtaining these supplies. Most of these supplies can be purchased at the pharmacy section of your local department store or at your local drug store pharmacy.

If you have trouble finding some of the supplies mentioned below, occasionally check for updates and information on my website at www.SurviveUntilTheEndComes.com about hard-to-find supplies as information becomes available.

Shown below are suggested quantities. You do not have to go out and purchase all these items at once. Just build up your kits a little at a time. When you purchase full boxes, you may have more or less of some items. This is NOT a medical or usage guide. This is a list of suggested supplies for someone trained and knowledgeable in their use. Here are the suggested lists "and quantities" for all three kits:

My Notes:

Primary Home First Aid Kit

[ ] (12) Canvas Triangular Bandages (non-sterile). These can be homemade from clean white bed linen sheets. To make triangular bandages from sheets, cut or rip an old full-size bed sheet in half which will give you two approximate pieces about 40" x 48". Bring one corner of the piece to the other corner to form a rough triangle. You now have a ready-to-use triangular bandage. You can continue to fold it corner to corner until you have a small roll that will easily fit in your first aid kit. Triangular bandages can be used for almost any purpose from tying a splint for a broken bone to making pressure bandages for severe bleeding. Add two large safety pins to each bandage to use for attaching the ends together to make slings and many other items. Learn how to use them well.

[ ] (12) 4" Self-Adhering White Sterile Gauze Rolls (also known as "Kling™ from Johnson & Johnson®")

[ ] (12) 3" Self-Adhering White Sterile Gauze Rolls (also known as "Kling™ from Johnson & Johnson®") (regular gauze rolls are much less effective than "Kling™ and must be taped)

[ ] (25) 4" x 4" Sterile Gauze Pads (also known as Gauze Sponges)

[ ] (25) 3" x 3" Sterile Gauze Pads (also known as Gauze Sponges)

[ ] (25) 3" x 3" Sterile Gauze Non-Stick Pads (for direct wound application)

[ ] (25) 2" x 2" Sterile Gauze Non-Stick Pads (for direct wound application)

[ ] (10) Large Eye Patches (these are usually coated so they do not stick)

[ ] (24) Large Butterfly Closure Strips (wound closure strips, usually in boxes)

[ ] (24) Wound Closure Strips (These are usually clear reinforced tape strips that adhere to bleeding wounds. These and butterfly bandages are used when sutures are not available to close wounds. Wounds should be thoroughly cleaned and washed with Betadine® Solution or other antiseptic prior to closure. Additional bandaging is required to keep these in place until the wound begins to heal. Several brand names are available. Ask a doctor or pharmacist.)

[ ] (20) Extra Large Peel-and-Stick Bandages (for large scrapes)

[ ] (20) Large Peel-and-Stick Bandages (for minor cuts)

[ ] (20) Large Waterproof 3M Nexcare™ (or equivalent) Clear Bandages. (These work very well on minor cuts. They seal even when wet and stay on until the wound is healed. Of course, you should clean and sterilize the wound before application with an antiseptic such as Betadine®.)

[ ] (3) Rolls 1/2" Medical Tape (designed to adhere to wet skin)

[ ] (3) Rolls 1" Medical Tape (designed to adhere to wet skin)

[ ] (6) Rolls 2" or 3" Sports Tape (This tape can be used with a little reinforcement to make a temporary field cast for a broken bone. It can also be used to tape up sprained ankles when walking is required. Just don't apply it so tightly that the circulation is reduced to the extremity.)

[ ] (6) Rolls 2" or 3" Sports Foam (for use under sports tape)

[ ] (6) Rolls of Heavy-Duty Mil Spec Duct Tape (buy a good quality name brand—many uses)

[ ] (3) 3' Lengths of Heavy-Duty Plastic Stretch Wrap (Many uses. Place in Ziploc® bags. Can be used to seal wounds and burns although non-sterile. Ask your first aid instructor about its uses.)

[ ] (3) 2' Long Sheets of Aluminum Foil (Add a same-size piece of heavy grade stretch wrap on top. Fold this into a small pack with the aluminum foil out. Place each of these in a Ziploc® type bag to keep them clean. You can place a sterile 4" x 4" gauze sponge with each pack. This pack unfolded makes a great seal for suctioning chest wounds. A sterile 4" x 4" gauze sponge is usually placed over the wound and this seal is placed over the gauze sponge, but ask your first aid instructor for proper use.)

[ ] (3) Petroleum Jelly-Covered Sterile Gauze Bandages (These are used as the aluminum foil and plastic wrap seals mentioned above, as well as burn dressings if sterile. You may have to get your first aid instructor to locate these for you or make your own.)

[ ] (10) Feet of Splint Wire (This is stiff woven wire or chicken wire with no more than 1/4" grids that have been cut into 4" wide by 2' long pieces. This can be purchased commercially for first aid kits, but you can obtain it from a local hardware store. You can wrap them in sports or first aid tape and fold or roll these up into small packages. They are used to help immobilize injured or broken bones. Don't put these directly next to the skin without putting a layer of gauze or cloth over the wire. Be sure the edges of the wire do not poke the skin. These can be molded to fit any need. Then tape them with sports tape or use triangular bandages to immobilize the injury. More than one piece can be used if necessary. Any stiff wire, soft flexible metal, or stiff cardboard can be used as a splint.)

[ ] (6) 6" ACE® or Equivalent Stretch Roll Bandages

[ ] (6) 4" ACE® or Equivalent Stretch Roll Bandages

[ ] (12) Trauma Dressings (These are large absorbent dressings designed to cover the entire chest, abdomen, or body. They make great additions to pressure dressings; however, these may also be used to hide the level of trauma rather than treat an injury. When someone has been multiply shot or run over by a truck, bleached white trauma dressings make it easier on the family and bystanders. Extra-large feminine hygiene pads are often used for trauma dressings. Don't laugh. Most ambulance services carry them as standard supplies. They are usually sterile and they are very absorbent).

[ ] (6) 20-oz Bottles of Distilled Water in Heavy Hard Plastic Bottles (used for washing wounds and hands)

[ ] (24) Pairs Sterile Disposable Gloves

[ ] (3) Emergency Blankets (pocket-size thin reflective foil - sold in camping supply sections)

[ ] (3) Emergency Blankets (heavy-duty laminated foil on tarp with grommets, usually 7' x 9')

[ ] (6) Pairs High Quality Surgical Hemostats (buy good ones that clamp tightly)

[ ] (3) Pairs of 6" High Quality, Medical Paramedic-Style Scissors (that will actually cut something)

[ ] (3) Pairs of High Quality Medical Tweezers (that will easily pick up a speck or a hair)

[ ] (6) Medical Quality Sterile Scalpels (X-ACTO® knives, if nothing else is available)

[ ] (12) Medical Quality Sterile Suture Kits (fine and medium)

[ ] (3) Rolls of Heavy-Duty Dental Floss (many uses)

[ ] (3) Stainless Steel Dental Probe Sets (available at automotive and hardware stores—not sterile)

[ ] (3) Small Handheld Non-Breakable Mirrors (about the size of a playing card)

[ ] (6) Top Quality BIC® Disposable Butane Lighters (don't use cheap ones - many uses, check often)

[ ] (1) OB Kit (obtainable from your ambulance service supply company - optional)

[ ] (6) Wooden Tongue Depressors (good for finger splints, too)

[ ] (6) Bottles of Sterile Eyewash (used for washing foreign objects from the eyes)

[ ] (6) Eyecups (for use with eyewash)

[ ] (3) Bottles each of Original and Moisture Restoring Eyedrops

[ ] (3) Small Boxes of Cotton-Tipped Ear Swabs (good for cleaning some wounds, too)

[ ] (1) Extractor Snakebite Kit (Made by Sawyer® and others, these look like a large syringe that draw in when you push the plunger down. They have several tips for use in snakebites and other medical needs when strong suction is required). Smaller pocket size snakebite kits can be used in the other kits where the danger exists.

[ ] (6) Penlights (check for operation often)

[ ] (3) Good Quality Aluminum Waterproof Flashlights (and extra batteries)

[ ] (6) Oral Thermometers

[ ] (6) Ice Packs (be careful not to crush them in the case)

[ ] (6) Hot Packs

[ ] (1) Bottle of Aspirin-Based Painkiller and Fever Reducer

[ ] (1) Bottle of Naproxen-Based Painkiller and Fever Reducer

[ ] (1) Bottle of Acetaminophen-Based Painkiller and Fever Reducer

[ ] (1) Bottle of Ibuprofen-Based Painkiller and Fever Reducer

[ ] (12) Single Use Packets of Aspirin (check expiration dates)

[ ] (12) Single Use Packets of Naproxen (check expiration dates)

[ ] (12) Single Use Packets of Acetaminophen (check expiration dates)

[ ] (12) Single Use Packets of Ibuprofen (check expiration dates)

[ ] (1) Bottle Anti-Diarrheal Liquid (extra strength)

[ ] (1) Bottle Pepto Bismol™ (for upset stomach)

[ ] (12) Single Use Packets of Anti-Diarrheal Pills

[ ] (12) Single Use Packets of Pepto Bismol™

[ ] (6) Packs of Acid Reducer such as Tums®, Rolaids®, or Maalox®

[ ] (6) Boxes of Non-Drowsy Formula Sinus Pills

[ ] (6) Boxes of Antihistamines for Sinus (usually causes drowsiness)

[ ] (6) Boxes of Benadryl® (may help with allergies and some allergic reactions and usually cause drowsiness)

[ ] (6) Boxes of Laxative Pills

[ ] (6) Bottles or Packs of Potassium Iodide Tablets (65mg or 130mg)

[ ] (6) 8-oz Bottles of Betadine® Solution Antiseptic (Povidone-Iodine 10%)

[ ] (6) 1-oz Tubes of Betadine® Ointment Maximum (Povidone-Iodine 10%) (Betadine® is probably the most used antiseptic in emergency rooms. It kills most bacteria and viruses, and may prevent infection in cuts and burns, and provides a protective barrier. The ointment is the same strength as the liquid and can be used in the smaller field kits. The liquid works well with wrapped dressings. Generic versions are available.)

[ ] (3) 1-oz Tubes Triple Antibiotic Ointment (good for minor cuts and burns)

[ ] (3) 1-oz Tubes Cortisone Cream

[ ] (6) Tubes of Sunblock (SPF 30 or higher)

[ ] (3) Bottles of Good Quality Insect Repellent

[ ] (6) Bottles of Burn Cream (designed to reduce pain and aid healing)

[ ] (3) Solar Showers (5-Gallon)

[ ] (3) Filter Masks N95 (designed to be used by a vehicle body painter. Get a good one that will filter pesticides and smoke particles)

[ ] (1) Full Face Gas or P100 Chemical Mask for each person. (filters at least 99.97% of airborne particles and is strongly resistant to oil) Buy a good one.

[ ] (1) Chemical Suit (This can be made from a full-body rain suit with all openings being duct taped. The full-face gas and chemical mask must also seal to the face and to the hood of the suit, and be sure any potential weak seal or opening is duct-taped closed.)

[ ] (1) Extra Pair of Vision or Reading Glasses for each person. Having some inexpensive (under $20) reading glasses (2:00 – 3:00 power) are great to have in your kit even if you don't currently need them. As we age, these magnifier glasses will come in handy, especially when doing close-up work like sewing up a cut. They will also have tremendous barter capability.

[ ] (1) First Aid Manual and Professional First Aid Training

There are some other items that you may deem usable once you get proper training. You might want a face mask and a set of airways for mouth-to-mouth resuscitation. These let you breathe into the victim's lungs without making contact with their lips. You might also want to include a supply of any medications you take regularly, but be sure and check the dates and rotate them often to keep them fresh. Talk to your doctor.

Once you have acquired the items listed above, you can begin to assemble your other kits. Let's begin with your "auto first aid kit." This kit is designed more for trauma than for sickness. You should remove the items from their original boxes for this kit. Do not open sterile wrappings. You can repackage similar items in heavy-duty Ziploc® clear plastic bags which come in pint, quart, and gallon sizes. Clearly label each bag with a Sharpie® with contents and date. These bags make your kit more organized and help keep the contents clean. You will need the following for this kit:

Custom Additions To This List:

[ ] _____

[ ] _____

[ ] _____

[ ] _____

[ ] _____

[ ] _____

[ ] _____

Auto First Aid Kit

(Made mostly from your large home kit with the addition of a few specialty items specific to the auto kit)

[ ] (4) Canvas/Linen Triangular Bandages

[ ] (4) 4" Self-Adhering White Sterile Gauze Rolls

[ ] (4) 3" Self-Adhering White Sterile Gauze Rolls

[ ] (8) 4" x 4" Sterile Gauze Pads

[ ] (8) 3" x 3" Sterile Gauze Pads

[ ] (8) 3" x 3" Sterile Gauze Non-Stick Pads

[ ] (8) 2" x 2" Sterile Gauze Non-Stick Pads

[ ] (2) Large Eye Patches

[ ] (8) Large Butterfly Closure Strips

[ ] (8) Wound Closure Strips

[ ] (8) Extra Large Peel-and-Stick Bandages for Large Scrapes

[ ] (8) Large Peel-and-Stick Bandages for Minor Cuts

[ ] (8) Large Waterproof 3M Nexcare™ Clear Bandages

[ ] (1) Roll 1/2" Medical Tape (designed to adhere to wet skin)

[ ] (1) Roll 1" Medical Tape (designed to adhere to wet skin)

[ ] (2) Rolls 2" or 3" Sports Tape (with rolls of foam)

[ ] (1) Roll of Heavy-Duty Highest Quality Mil Spec Duct Tape

[ ] (1) 3' Length of Heavy-Duty Plastic Stretch Wrap

[ ] (1) 2' Long Sheet of Aluminum Foil

[ ] (1) Petroleum Jelly-Covered Sterile Gauze Bandage

[ ] (3) Feet of Splint Wire

[ ] (2) 6" ACE® or Equivalent Stretch Roll Bandages

[ ] (2) 4" ACE® or Equivalent Stretch Roll Bandages

[ ] (2) Trauma Dressings or Large Feminine Hygiene Pads

[ ] (1) 20-oz Bottle of Distilled Water for Cleaning

[ ] (4) Pairs Sterile Disposable Gloves

[ ] (1) Emergency Blanket (pocket-size)

[ ] (1) Pair High Quality Surgical Hemostats

[ ] (1) Pair of 6" High Quality, Medical Paramedic-Style Scissors

[ ] (1) Pair of High Quality Medical Tweezers

[ ] (1) Medical Quality Scalpel

[ ] (2) Medical Quality Suture Kits

[ ] (1) Roll of Heavy-Duty Dental Floss

[ ] (1) Stainless Steel Dental Probe Set

[ ] (1) Small Handheld Non-Breakable Mirror

[ ] (1) Top Quality BIC® Disposable Butane Lighter (check operation often)

[ ] (2) Wooden Tongue Depressors

[ ] (1) Bottle of Sterile Eyewash

[ ] (1) Eyecup (for use with eyewash—usually comes with the wash as a kit)

[ ] (1) Small Bottle Each of Original and Moisture Restoring Eyedrops

[ ] (1) Small Box of Cotton-Tipped Ear Swabs

[ ] (1) Snakebite Kit (Small ones sold in camping sections)

[ ] (1) Penlight (check operation often)

[ ] (1) Good Quality Aluminum Waterproof Flashlight (and extra batteries)

[ ] (1) Oral Thermometer

[ ] (2) Ice Packs

[ ] (2) Hot Packs

[ ] (4) Single Use Packets of Aspirin (check expiration dates)

[ ] (4) Single Use Packets of Naproxen (check expiration dates)

[ ] (4) Single Use Packets of Acetaminophen (check expiration dates)

[ ] (4) Single Use Packets of Ibuprofen (check expiration dates)

[ ] (4) Single Use Packets of Anti-Diarrheal Pills

[ ] (4) Single Use Packets of Pepto Bismol™

[ ] (1) Pack of Acid Reducer such as Tums®, Rolaids®, or Maalox®

[ ] (1) Box of Non-Drowsy Formula Sinus Pills

[ ] (1) Box of Antihistamines for Sinus

[ ] (1) Box of Benadryl®

[ ] (1) Box of Laxative Pills

[ ] (1) 8-oz Bottle of Betadine® Solution Antiseptic (Povidone-Iodine 10%)

[ ] (2) 1-oz Tubes of Betadine® Ointment Maximum (Povidone-Iodine 10%)

[ ] (1) 1-oz Tube Triple Antibiotic Ointment

[ ] (1) 1-oz Tube Cortisone Cream

[ ] (1) Tube of Sunblock (SPF 30 or higher)

[ ] (1) Bottle of Good Quality Insect Repellent

[ ] (1) Bottle of Burn Cream

[ ] (1) Solar Shower (3-5 Gallon)

[ ] (1) Extra pair of vision or reading glasses

[ ] (1) First Aid Manual and Professional First Aid Training

Custom Additions To This List:

[ ] _____

[ ] _____

[ ] _____

[ ] _____

[ ] _____

[ ] _____

[ ] _____

[ ] _____

[ ] _____

Travel or Personal First Aid Kit (Bug-Out Kit)

[ ] (4) Canvas/Linen Triangular Bandages

[ ] (4) 4" Self-Adhering White Sterile Gauze Rolls

[ ] (4) 3" Self-Adhering White Sterile Gauze Rolls

[ ] (8) 4" x 4" Sterile Gauze Pads

[ ] (8) 3" x 3" Sterile Gauze Pads

[ ] (8) 3" x 3" Sterile Gauze Non-Stick Pads

[ ] (8) 2" x 2" Sterile Gauze Non-Stick Pads

[ ] (2) Large Eye Patches

[ ] (4) Large Butterfly Closure Strips

[ ] (4) Wound Closure Strips

[ ] (4) Extra Large Peel-and-Stick Bandages for Large Scrapes

[ ] (4) Large Peel-and-Stick Bandages for Minor Cuts

[ ] (4) Large Waterproof 3M Nexcare™ (or equivalent) Clear Bandages

[ ] (1) Roll 1/2" Medical Tape (designed to adhere to wet skin)

[ ] (1) Roll 1" Medical Tape (designed to adhere to wet skin)

[ ] (2) Rolls 2" or 3" Sports Tape with foam

[ ] (1) Roll of Heavy-Duty Mil Spec Duct Tape

[ ] (1) 3' Length of Heavy-Duty Plastic Stretch Wrap

[ ] (1) 3' Long Sheet of Heavy-Duty Aluminum Foil

[ ] (1) Petroleum Jelly-Covered Sterile Gauze Bandage

[ ] (3) Feet of Splint Wire

[ ] (2) 6" ACE® or Equivalent Stretch Roll Bandages

[ ] (2) 4" ACE® or Equivalent Stretch Roll Bandages

[ ] (4) Trauma Dressings or Large Feminine Hygiene Pads

[ ] (1) 20-oz Bottle of Distilled Water for Cleaning

[ ] (4) Pair Sterile Disposable Gloves

[ ] (1) Emergency Blanket (pocket-size)

[ ] (1) Pair High Quality Surgical Hemostats

[ ] (1) Pair of 6" High Quality, Medical Paramedic-Style Scissors

[ ] (1) Pair of High Quality Medical Tweezers

[ ] (1) Medical Quality Scalpel

[ ] (2) Medical Quality Suture Kit

[ ] (1) Stainless Steel Dental Probe Set

[ ] (1) Roll of Heavy-Duty Dental Floss

[ ] (1) Small Handheld Non-Breakable Mirror

[ ] (1) Top Quality BIC® Disposable Butane Lighter (check operation often)

[ ] (2) Wooden Tongue Depressors

[ ] (1) Bottle of Sterile Eyewash

[ ] (1) Eyecup (for use with eyewash—usually comes with the wash as a kit)

[ ] (1) Small Bottle of Original and Moisture Restoring Eyedrops

[ ] (1) Small Box of Cotton-Tipped Ear Swabs

[ ] (1) Snakebite Kit (small ones sold in camping sections)

[ ] (1) Penlight (check operation often)

[ ] (1) Good Quality Aluminum Waterproof Flashlight (and extra batteries)

[ ] (1) Oral Thermometer

[ ] (1) Ice Pack

[ ] (1) Hot Pack

[ ] (4) Single Use Packets of Aspirin (check expiration dates)

[ ] (4) Single Use Packets of Naproxen (check expiration dates)

[ ] (4) Single Use Packets of Acetaminophen (check expiration dates)

[ ] (4) Single Use Packets of Ibuprofen (check expiration dates)

[ ] (4) Single Use Packets of Anti-Diarrheal Pills

[ ] (4) Single Use Packets of Pepto Bismol™

[ ] (1) Pack of Acid Reducer such as Tums®, Rolaids®, or Maalox®

[ ] (1) Box of Non-Drowsy Formula Sinus Pills

[ ] (1) Box of Antihistamines for Sinus

[ ] (1) Box of Benadryl®

[ ] (1) Box of Laxative Pills

[ ] (1) 1-oz Tube of Betadine® Ointment Maximum (Povidone-Iodine 10%)

[ ] (1) 1-oz Tube Triple Antibiotic Ointment

[ ] (1) 1-oz Tube Cortisone Cream

[ ] (1) Tube of Sunblock (SPF 30 or higher)

[ ] (1) Bottle of Good Quality Insect Repellent

[ ] (1) Bottle of Burn Cream

[ ] (1) Extra Pair of Vision or Reading Glasses

[ ] (1) First Aid Guide and Professional First Aid Training

Custom Additions To This List:

[ ] _____

[ ] _____

[ ] _____

[ ] _____

[ ] _____

[ ] _____

[ ] _____

[ ] _____

[ ] _____

[ ] _____

[ ] _____

[ ] _____

The balance of the supplies after stocking your auto and personal or travel (bug-out) first aid kits goes into your primary home (or bunker) first aid kit. Remember, if you are at home, the travel kit and the auto kit will likely be there, too; so if a survival event occurs while you are at home, be sure and pull the three kits together in case you need them. Take all three kits to your bunker or bug-out location which may become your home for a long time. You can also construct a small essentials kit for carrying in your pocket or purse.

Keep your kits updated and clean. Replace items as used or if dates expire. Learn how to use everything in the kit. Better still, learn how to make your own supplies should these run out. Learn to make triangular bandages from linens. They are simple to make. Take a clean bed sheet or roll of muslin (preferably white) and cut a square approximately 5' x 5'. Fold one corner over to another. This now becomes a triangle. This can be used, as is, as a sling, head dressing or to hold a dressing on the chest. Fold it down into a 3" wide bandage and it can be used as a compression bandage, a tourniquet, or to tie on splints. It is one of the most commonly used dressings when commercial dressings are not available.

In the old days, these bandages and other tools used in medicine were boiled or steamed to kill most of the germs on them. Since antibiotics may not be available in a survival situation, cleanliness will become very important. Wash your hands before you perform first aid on yourself or others. Use sterile procedures and supplies when possible. Try to sterilize bandages and instruments with steam or by boiling if possible. Use products designed to prevent infection such as Betadine® when available. Wear sterile disposable gloves if you have them to protect you and others. Learn how to protect yourself from airborne viruses and biological and chemical threats, too. See step-by-step instructions with photos in my book (published 2013) *"Survive Until The End Comes"* www.SurviveUntilTheEndComes.com. Take your first aid classes and learn how to apply aid to yourself and others. Your first aid skills and knowledge may become more valuable to you than gold when other unskilled and untrained people need your help.

Summary

The *"Survival Preppers Doomsday Survival Checklist"* once completed, should get you through the first three hours after the survival event, the trip from work to home or your bunker when disaster strikes, and the ability to survive for the first thirty days until you develop a sufficiency to survive for the long-term. This checklist is designed to be utilized at the moment of disaster and as an aid to developing three complete survival and first aid kits prior to disaster occurring. This list is a product of over eight years of survival and first aid research and years of medical rescue field experience. The year 2015 is upon us and the world seems to be imploding on itself.

I truly hope the events I discussed in my book *"Survive Until The End Comes"* never occur. The problem is, as I finished the second edition and the bug-out edition of the book in 2013, there are, or have been, record-breaking earthquakes, comets, tornadoes, hurricanes, volcanoes, fires, droughts, oil well disasters, shootings, wars, Ebola, childhood diseases that resemble a form of Polio, and other disasters in unlikely places occurring on an increasing and more severe level. There are starving people around the world, and it's getting worse. The world economies seem to be on the verge of collapsing. Evil and chaos are growing. Chaos seems to be occurring on the streets of America. Few call on the name of God anymore. People still ask me if it will happen. It is happening, daily!

Many individuals are suffering personal financial problems that they have never suffered before. We are at war in the Middle East and probably several other places. Syria seems to be in total civil war; and who is ISIS? No one seems to know what Venezuela is up to. They do not seem to like us very much. North Korea is telling us, almost daily, that they are going to send a nuke to America. Iran made a statement recently that it was now producing high-quality weapons' grade uranium, but they always tell us it's for electricity purposes. Iran is one of the world's largest producers of oil. Does Iran really need nuclear reactors to produce electricity? They call America "The Great Satan". Chaos is here. American soldiers are still dying everyday. Is World War III just around the corner? Fuel hit record highs, dropped and still dropping. Third World people are starving and fighting, and superpowers are suffering from the bad economy and bad weather. I believe wars will increase and I believe world war and total chaos is possible. Should I even mention Ukraine and Russia? And what about Africa?

Can we survive? Mankind has always survived. Humans, since Adam and Eve, have survived: floods, famines, wars, and evil of all sorts, disease, plagues, depressions, the space age, and television. Millions have died in the process, but with what I believe to be God's help, we have continued on. Could the end be near for humanity? If Almighty God is about to bring time to an end, there is nothing that I know of that I, or anyone else, can do to stop it. God gave us minds and the ability to use our minds to put our hands and feet to use. God, I believe, gave us knowledge and wisdom. It is up to us to use these gifts. We can sit around and wait, or we can do all we can to survive as long as possible. Without God, this book would not exist. All power, glory, and honor go to God. I would like to thank my dear wife, Deborah. Without her excellent proofing abilities, her patience, and her motivation, I could never have made this work presentable to the public.

Thank you for purchasing the *"Survival Preppers Doomsday Survival Checklist"*. Get started on building your kits today! Practice and develop basic skills that you may need someday soon to save your life or your loved ones' lives. Almighty God gave me the ability to write; I now give this information to you, the reader. You decided to open it and study its pages. It is now your job to pass anything you may have learned along to your loved ones. Learn basic first aid. Study other survival books, including ones dedicated to outdoor survival skills. I also suggest you read the Bible, both the Old and New Testaments. You will read how people survived many bad situations. Remember, that our greatest enemy can become ourselves. Most importantly, I hope you "survive until the end comes!" May God's Almighty will be done.